KAPPIYA'S RECIPE IDEAS- 1

BACHELORS COOK TABLE

KAPPIYA CLASSICS

Made with ♥ on the Notion Press Platform
www.notionpress.com

Contents

Foreword *v*

1. Pepper Rasam 1
2. Tomato Rasam 2
3. RASAM RICE 5
4. Mushroom Peas Pulao 7
5. Ven Pongal 8
6. Semiya Pongal 9
7. Rava Pongal 10
8. Simple Dal 11
9. Pasipayaru Sambar 12
10. Sambar 14
11. Tomato Semiya 16
12. Curd Semiya 18
13. Rava Upma 19
14. Bread Upma 21
15. Oats Upma 23
16. Masala Poha 25
17. Tomato Rice 27
18. Lemon Rice 28
19. Corn Mushroom Fried Rice 29
20. Flattened Rice (Aval, Poha) 31
21. Rava Dosa 32
22. Bread Dosai 33
23. Kadalai Mavu Dosai 34
24. Paneer Masala Dosai 35
25. Egg Roll 37
26. Mint Pasta 38
27. Egg Dosa 40

Contents

28. Adai Dosa 41

29. Moong Dal Dosa 42

30. Ragi Dosa 44

31. Coconut Chutney 48

32. Tomato Chutney 49

33. EGG THOKKU 50

34. Egg Pepper Fry 52

35. Pepper Chicken 53

36. Cabbage With Moong Dal 55

37. POTATO FRY 56

38. EGGPLANT CURRY 57

39. Avial 58

40. Onion Pakoda 59

41. Green Peas Masala 60

42. Kara Boondhi Kurma 62

43. Rajma Curry 64

44. Potato Curry 65

45. Moong (Green Gram) Gravy 66

46. Tomato Sweet Pachadi 67

47. Mixed Vegetable Curd Pachadi 68

48. Carrot Kosumalli 69

49. Green Chili Pachadi 71

50. Popcorn 73

Foreword

KAPPIYA CLASSICS

Hello Dear Readers

I am Tamizhiniya Tamizhdesan

when I was studying in school my teachers used to conduct lessons between many good books and that conduct gave me confidence that I can conduct more than a hundred topics with introductory speech. My Technical education helped a lot in this aspect. When I became a teacher I assisted my students in the way our teachers guided us.

My school, college and workplace friends lives scattered in different countries, the families of them too scattered in different nation, whereas I live in the Land of my Mother Language(Tamilnadu). Among my friends who are running to strive for their living, I have selected the publishing department to read their lives and pass it on to others. We are publishing legendary works under Kappiya Vasipagam. So far we have published more than 1500 books in package type.

I have used the library a lot in my school, college and work life. Novelist Vasu Murugavel writes that he brought a bundle of books from a person, read them and returned them. Similarly, I have imported hundreds of books read them and sent them back. I have also written novel in Tamil and English, also a book based on the Culture of Tamil People.

My son Imayakappiyan (8) started learning his Tamil lettering from the texts of our cover pages. The same way he is gaining the knowledge of book names, authors also the technical knowledge in publishing and helps us in many ways. My husband Tamizhdesan guides me about the packaging materials of the book contents and his creative thinking of book cover page makes me to create some unique cover pages. We three feel very happy to be in this field which makes us to learn continuously.

1

Pepper Rasam

Ingredients:

Tomatoes - 2
Tamarind paste
Salt
Pepper
Asafoetida
Coriander leaves

Preparation:

Cut the tomatoes and add tamarind paste. Put some pepper and salt and grind it in the blender. Heat water in a vessel and add this paste to it. when it starts boiling, Add asafoetida powder and a little more salt and pepper and stir well for 3 minutes. Simmer stove, add coriander leaves and bring it to boil again and switch off stove. Spicy rasam is ready.

A couple of cloves of garlic may be added for tastier rasam.

2

Tomato Rasam

Ingredients You Need

For tomato rasam, we use cumin seeds and black pepper as the main spices. You can increase or decrease the proportion of pepper to adjust with your taste and desired level of spice.

Other ingredients that are needed are tender coriander stems (cilantro, with or without leaves), ginger and garlic. Again, feel free to use more or less ginger and garlic depending on how fragrant you want your dish.

Plus you also need, of course, juicy red tomatoes and plenty of Indian spices and herbs.

How to make Tomato Rasam

Make Ground Herbs And Spice Mixture

1. To a blender or food processor add ⅓ cup (about a handful) of roughly chopped coriander stems, with or without leaves. Add 7 to 8 medium sized garlic cloves, peeled, and 1 inch of peeled ginger, roughly chopped.(If not in blender you can use a hand pound to crush those)

2. Add 2 teaspoons of cumin seeds and ¼ teaspoon of whole black peppercorns. Feel free to use less or more pepper to taste.

3. Grind to a coarse paste, but do not puree. Transfer the paste to a bowl or plate and set aside.

Making Tomato Puree

4. To the same blender jar add 3 large ripe and red tomatoes, rinsed and chopped. You will need 275 grams tomatoes, or roughly 1.5 to 1.75 cups of chopped tomatoes.

5. Blend the tomatoes to a smooth puree. For a beautiful bright red rasam, you can first blanch the tomatoes and then puree them.

(To blanch tomatoes, boil them in a pot of water for one to two minutes before quickly plunging in a bath of ice water. This stops the cooking process and keeps the tomatoes super red and juicy.)

Fry The Spices, Herbs

6. In a heavy pan or pot, heat 2 tablespoons oil on low heat. Once the oil is hot add ½ teaspoon of mustard seeds.

You can use gingelly oil (made from raw sesame seeds) or sunflower, peanut or any neutral oil.

7. Fry the mustard seeds until they begin to crackle.

8. Next add ½ teaspoon of urad dal (lentils).

While the dal adds great texture and taste, feel free to leave them out if you don't like them or don't have any on hand.

9. Continue to stir often as you fry the urad dal to a golden brown.

10. Add 1 to 2 dry red chilies (halved and seeds removed), and 1 pinch asafoetida (hing). Turn the heat off if the pot gets too hot and nearly smokes.

11. Stir and fry the chilies for few seconds, until they start to lose their red color and become reddish brown.

12. Add the coarsely ground coriander, ginger, cumin, black pepper and garlic paste to the pan. Again, if the pan is so hot that anything begins to burn, promptly turn the heat off and/or remove the pan from the stove.

13. Now add 10 to 12 curry leaves, whole or chopped.

14. Sauté for a minute on low, being careful to not burn the spices.

15. Add ¼ teaspoon of turmeric powder.

16. Stir to thoroughly blend the turmeric powder in with the spice mixture.

17. Carefully add the tomato puree.

18. Mix well. The tomato rasam will almost immediately smell amazing.

19. Continue to stir and simmer for a minute to heat the mixture through.

20. Season with salt to taste.

21. Next add 1.5 cups of water, and stir. If you want a thinner soup you can add a splash more water. But I don't recommend adding too much more, or you risk diluting the delicious flavors of the thakkali rasam.

22. Increase the temperature to medium-low heat and bring the soup to a gently boil. Stir again, and reduce the heat back down to low.

23. Simmer for about 10 minutes, stirring occassionally.

24. Turn off the heat and add 2 tablespoons of chopped coriander (cilantro) leaves. Taste, and add more salt if needed.

Serving Tomato Rasam

Serve tomato rasam or thakkali rasam hot, either like a curry over steamed white rice or enjoy as a bowl of hearty soup. Both ways are great with a side of pappadums or simple toasted bread.

Storage

Refrigerate any leftovers for a day. Reheat the tomato rasam in a small pot or pan until warm or hot. If you plan to make ahead the thakkali rasam then do not add coriander leaves. After you reheat rasam, add the coriander leaves.

Helpful Tips

Tomatoes: Tomato rasam is best made with fresh, red, ripe tomatoes. Any variety of red tomatoes work, provided they are ripe.

Spices: For a spicy and robust thakkali rasam, increase the amount of whole black peppercorns by adding a total of ½ teaspoon.

Oil: Traditionally in the Tamil Nadu cuisine, rasam is made with gingelly oil. This gingelly oil is nothing but wood pressed oil extracted from raw sesame seeds. In a pinch you can opt to use sunflower oil, peanut oil or any neutral oil.

3

RASAM RICE

INGREDIENTS

1 cup = 250ml

Raw rice or Steamed rice - 1/2 cup

Toor dal - 1 tbsp

Water - 2.5 cups

Salt - as needed

Ripe tomato - 1 (finely chopped)

Tamarind - Small gooseberry size

Turmeric Powder - 1/4 tsp

Rasam Powder or sambar powder - 1/2 tsp

To temper

Ghee - 1 tbsp

Mustard seeds - 1/2 tsp

Asafoetida / Hing - 1/4 tsp

Pepper Cumin Powder - 1 tsp

Crushed garlic – 4 cloves

Red Chilli - 1

Green Chilli - 1

Curry Leaves - Few

Coriander Leaves - to garnish

PREPARATION:

Wash the rice and toor dal. Add water and soak till use or around 30 minutes.

Heat ghee in a pressure cooker base. Splutter mustard seeds, hing, curry leaves, red chilli and green chilli.

Add a tsp of pepper cumin powder, garlic and saute for a minute.

Now add the tomato and saute till mushy. Add sambar or rasam powder.

Add 1/2 cup of tamarind extract. turmeric powder, salt and mix well. Lastly add the soaked rice and toor dal. Add 2.5 cups water and required salt.

Pressure cook in low flame for 2 whistles. Switch off the flame and allow the pressure to release naturally.

Open the cooker and mix well. Garnish with coriander leaves.

Enjoy with potato curry and papad.

Note:

Adjust the quantity of water as per your need.

Do not skip pepper cumin powder. It helps to give nice flavor.

Add rasam powder for typical rasam rice taste.

4

Mushroom Peas Pulao

INGREDIENTS

1. 1 cup - 250ml
2. Mushroom - 10 nos
3. Green peas or dried peas - 1/4 cup
4. Basmati Rice - 1 cup
5. Water or coconut milk - 1.75 cups
6. Cooking oil+ Ghee - 2 tbsp + 1 tbsp
7. Cinnamon - 1 inch, Cloves - 2 nos, Cardamom - 1 no
8. Black stone flower/ Kalpasi - 2 small
9. Fennel seeds - 1/4 tsp
10. Bay leaf – 1 no
11. Big onion - 1 no
12. Ginger Garlic Paste - 1.5 tsp
13. Green chilli - 3 nos (Use 2 for less spice)
14. Mint leaves - a handful
15. Salt - as needed/Lemon juice – Few drops

PREPARATION: Wash and clean mushroom. Slice it and set aside. Heat oil + ghee in a cooker. Saute whole garam masala. Add onion, Ginger Garlic Paste paste, green chilli, mint leaves and saute till transparent. Add mushroom, peas and saute for a minute. Add rice, saute for a minute. Lastly add water or coconut milk and mix well. Pressure cook in low flame for one whistle.

5

Ven Pongal

It is also a nice comforting and healthy food for the babies, because of its soft texture.

Ingredients

1 cup BASMATI RICE or Any variety Raw rice

0.25 cup MOONG DAL

2 tbsp GHEE

1 tsp CUMIN SEED

2 tsp PEPPER BLACK

0.25 tsp HING OR ASAFOETIDA

5 no CURRY LEAVES

5 no CASHEW NUTS RAW

1 tsp GINGER GRATED

Method

Wash and soak the rice and moong dal together for 20 minutes.

In a pressure cooker add 4 cups of water, salt, chopped ginger and cook it for 4 whistles. Allow the pressure cooker to cool naturally.

In a skillet heat ghee, add black pepper, cumin seeds and allow it to splutter.

Remove the skillet from heat, add cashew nuts and roast until the color changes into golden brown.

Add curry leaves, asafoetida, mix well in the ghee, add to the rice and dal mixture. Mix well and serve with plain sambar or coconut chutney.

6

Semiya Pongal

INGREDIENTS

Vermicelli (Semiya) – One big bowl (100 grams)
Green Gram (Moong) Dal – 1/4 cup (50 grams)
Turmeric Powder – a pinch
Black Pepper – 2 teaspoons
Cumin (Jeeragam) – 1 teaspoon
Fresh Ginger – a small piece
Ghee – 1 tablespoon
Asafotida Powder – 2 pinches
Cashewnuts – few
Green Chili – 1
Curry Leaves – few
Salt – 1 teaspoon or as per taste

Method

In a kadai put a teaspoon of ghee and add semiya. Fry till it slightly turns light brown. Remove and keep it aside.

Coarsely powder the pepper and cumin. Finely chop the ginger. Just give a slit to the green chilli.

Wash the Green Gram (Moong) Dal and add four cups of water. Add a pinch of turmeric powder, finely chopped ginger and cook it. Once it is $3/4^{th}$ cooked, add the fried semiya (vermicelli) along with salt. Stir well and close with a lid. Cook on low flame till all the water is absorbed and the semiya is cooked well.

In a kadai put the ghee and when it is hot add cashew nuts, asafotida powder, pepper and cumin powder, slit green cchilli and curry leaves. Pour this seasoning to the cooked semiya and mix well.

7

Rava Pongal

Ingredients needed

1. Rava - 1 cup
2. Moong dal (pasi paruppu) - 1/3 cup
3. Ginger finely chopped - 1 tsp
4. Whole black pepper - 1 tsp
5. Cumin seeds/Jeera - 1 tsp
6. Chille - 1 finely chopped
7. Ghee - 1/4 cup
8. Cashew nuts - 3
9. Salt as required

Preparation: Roast rava in a tsp of ghee till it becomes hot to touch. Do not over roast it.

Cook moong dal till soft.(DON'T MAKE IT MUSHY)

Crush cumin seeds and pepper coarsely.

Method: Heat ghee in a pan, add finely chopped ginger, grounded pepper+ cumin seeds, cashew nuts and curry leaves. Saute for a few seconds, then add 2 cups of boiling water. Add salt to taste. Simmer the flame and then slowly add rava, stirring continuously. After the rava gets cooked, add the cooked moong dal and cook till all the water evaporates.

Eat hot with coconut chutney or sambar.

8

Simple Dal

Ingredients:

1. 1/2 cup Masoor Dal
2. 1 Tomato
3. 1/2 tsp Jeera
4. 1/4 tsp Turmeric powder
5. 2 Green chillies
6. 3 tsp Oil
7. 1 level tsp Salt
8. 3 Garlic Cloves
9. Coriander leaves

Preparation:

Cook the dal with salt, turmeric powder and slit green chillies in a pan or pressure cooker.

In another pan, heat oil, add the jeera, tomatoes and garlic pods, saute on a high flame till the tomatoes are soft and pulpy.

Add the cooked dal into this with little water, boil well for 15 minutes to incorporate the masala into the dal. Garnish with coriander leaves.

This dish goes well with plain white rice or chapathi/ roti

9

Pasipayaru Sambar

1 cup = 250 ml cup

Ingredients :

1/2 cup moong dal/pasipayaru/payatham paruppu

250 gms Ashgourd/white pumpkin (peeled and cubed)

2 tomatoes (chopped)

gooseberry size tamarind (soak in 1/2 cup warm water for 10 minutes and extract juice)

1 tablespoon sambar powder (adjust)

1/4 teaspoon turmeric powder

salt to taste

For tempering :

2 teaspoons sesame oil

1 teaspoon mustard seeds

1/4 teaspoon methi/fenugreek seeds

pinch of asafoetida

1 sprig curry leaves

For garnish : finely chopped coriander leaves

Method :

1. Heat a pan/pressure pan with sesame oil and temper with ingredients given.

2. Add the tomatoes and ash gourd , add turmeric, salt and saute' them for 2-3 minutes .

3. Now add the extracted tamarind juice , sambar powder , moong dal(uncooked) and mix well.

4. Adjust the water quantity (add approximately 1 cup of water) and pressure cook the sambar for upto 3 whistles and switch off.

5. Once the pressure releases, open the pressure cooker and using a hand whisk (I use my wooden Mathu) whisk the dal carefully without mashing the ash gourd.

6. Garnish with coriander leaves .

10

Sambar

South Indian Sambar is a delicious curry with softly boiled and mashed lentil and vegetables. It is a traditional South Indian dish served with rice.

Ingredients

1 cup Toor Dal

1 cup Onion Chopped

2 no Tomatoes

1 tsp Tamarind Paste or one tablespoon raw tamarind

15 no Okra (Can add any vegetables as per wish)

2 tbsp Sambar Powder

1/2 tsp Mustard Seeds

1 tsp Urad Dal

1/2 tsp Asafoetida

10 no Curry Leaves

2 tbsp Oil

2 no Green Chilies

1/2 tsp Turmeric Powder

2 tsp Salt (to taste)

1 tsp Fenugreek Seeds

Method

Rinse toor dal with water 3 to 4 times until the water runs clear.

In a pressure cooker, add toor dal, water, salt, turmeric powder and cook for 4 whistles and let the pressure cooker cool naturally. Uncover the pressure cooker and mash the dal using the back of a ladle.

In a saucepan, heat oil, add fenugreek seeds and saute until the color changes to light brown. Add mustard seeds and allow to splutter. Add urad dal and saute until the color changes to golden brown.

Add asafoetida (hing) and mix well in the oil. Add chopped onion, curry leaves, green chilies and cook until the onion becomes soft.

Add chopped okra, sprinkle little amount of water and cook until the okra becomes soft.

Add chopped tomatoes and cook until the tomatoes become soft.

Add tamarind paste, water, mix well and bring to a boil. Add sambar powder and boil until the sambar powder loses its raw smell.

Add mashed dal, salt and mix well. Bring the sambar to a boil and garnish with chopped coriander leaves. Sambar is ready to serve.

11

Tomato Semiya

INGREDIENTS

Semiya (Vermicelli) – 2 cups
Tomato – 2/Onion – 1
Green Chilli – 1/Red Chilli – 1
Garlic Flakes – 4
Red Chilli Powder – 1/2 teaspoon
Turmeric Powder – 1/4 teaspoon
Oil – 2 to 3 tablespoons
Mustrad – 1/2 teaspoon
Curry Leaves – few
Cashew Nuts – few (optional)
Salt – 1/2 teaspoon or as per taste

Method

Boil 6 cups of water along with a teaspoon of oil and salt. Add semiya (vermicelli) and cook till it is soft. Remove from stove and drain the excess water. Immediately add cold water and rinse well. Drain all the water completely and put the cooked semiya in a plate.

Chop onion, garlic and tomato finely. Slit green chilli lengthwise.

In a thick bottomed kadai put the oil. When it is hot add mustard. When the mustard starts popping up add red chilli, curry leaves, chopped garlic and fry till the garlic turn light brown.

Then add chopped onion and fry for few seconds. Put chopped tomato and fry for few more seconds and then green chillies, turmeric powder and fry till tomatoes are mashed well.

Add red chilli powder and salt. Stir well.

Add cooked semiya (Vermicelli) and mix thoroughly.

Add fried cashew nuts and remove.
Serve with any Curd Pachadi or with plain curd (Yogurt).

12

Curd Semiya

Ingredients needed

1. Vermicelli - 1/2 cup
2. Milk - 1/2 cup
3. Curd - 1 cup /Water -1 1/2 cup

For the seasoning

1. Oil - 1 1/2 tsp
2. Mustard - 1 tsp
3. Asafoetida/ hing - a pinch
4. Ginger - 1 inch piece finely chopped
5. Green chilli - 1 finely chopped
6. Curry leaves - few

For garnishing (optional) (Use any one)
Grated carrots / Pomegranates/ Green seedless grapes/ Cashew nuts.

Method: Cook semiya in boiling water adding salt and a tsp of oil. Stir now and then to prevent it from forming lumps. After it is cooked, add milk stirring continuously. Remove from flame. Allow it to cool. Then add curd and mix well. Heat a tsp of oil, add mustard seeds, when it splutters, add hing, ginger, green chillies, curry leaves and saute for a few seconds. Add to the semiya. Garnish with coriander leaves and any one of the above mentioned in garnishing.

13

Rava Upma

Prep and Roast Rava

1. Prep the ingredients first to make upma recipe. Take 1 cup rava (fine variety) and set it aside.

⅓ cup finely chopped onions

1 teaspoon chopped green chillies

1 teaspoon finely chopped ginger

2 tablespoons coriander leaves (cilantro)

8 to 10 curry leaves

10 to 12 cashews (optional)

1 teaspoon chana dal (hulled and split bengal gram)

1 teaspoon urad dal (hulled and split black gram)

2. Heat a pan or kadai first. Add 1 cup rava or cream of wheat (fine variety).

3. Begin to roast the rava. Stir often while roasting the rava.

4. The rava or sooji grains should become fragrant and start to look dry, separate and crisp. Don't brown the rava.

5. Once the rava becomes fragrant and starts to look dry and crisp, switch off the flame and put the roasted rava on a plate and set aside.

Fry and Sauté

5. In a pan, heat 2 tablespoons ghee (clarified butter) or oil. You could use sunflower oil or peanut oil or any neutral tasting oil.

7. Lower the heat. Add 1 teaspoon mustard seeds. When you hear the crackling sound of mustard seeds, it means they are getting fried.

8. Now add the ½ teaspoon cumin seeds along with 1 teaspoon chana dal (husked and split bengal gram) and 1 teaspoon urad dal (husked and split black gram).

9. Stirring often fry until the chana dal and urad dal begin to brown a bit.

10. Immediately add 10 to 12 cashews and begin to fry on a low to medium-low heat.

11. By the time the cashews get golden the dals should also be golden.

12. Now add the finely chopped onions.

13. Sauté the onions until they soften and become translucent on a low to medium-low heat.

14. Then add the chopped green chillies, ginger and curry leaves. You can also add 1 dried red chilli (halved and with seeds removed) at this step.

15. Mix well & sauté for a few seconds.

Boil Water

16. Then add 2.5 cups water to this mixture.

17. Add salt as required. Mix well and check the taste of water. It should be a bit salty but not too much.

In case if the salt becomes less in the dish, you can always sprinkle some salt from the top when eating.

19. Stir again. On a medium to high flame, heat the water and let it come to a rolling boiling.

Make Rava Upma

20. When the water comes to a rolling boil, lower the flame to its lowest. Then add the rava in 4 to 5 batches with a spoon.

21. Once you add the first batch of rava, stir and mix immediately so that the roasted rava gets mixed evenly with the water.

22. Then add the next batch of rava. Mix and stir again very well ensuring that the batch of rava is mixed evenly in water.

23. Continue to add and stir the rava up to the last batch.

24. Quickly stir and mix very well. The rava grains will absorb water, swell and get cooked.

25. Cover and allow the rava upma to steam for 2 to 3 minutes on a low heat.

26. Then switch off the heat. In the below photo, the rava is cooked well and the suji ka upma is ready.

27. Lastly add about 2 tablespoons chopped coriander leaves (cilantro). You can add more coriander leaves if you like.

28. Mix again.

14

Bread Upma

Preparation time : 10 minutes

Cooking time : 15 -20 minutes

Serves : 4

1 cup = 250 ml

Ingredients :

10 slices of bread (chopped)

1 large onion (finely chopped)

2 tomatoes (finely chopped)

1/4 cup green peas

1/2 " ginger (grated or finely chopped)

15-20 moringa leaves (optional)

1/2 capsicum (finely chopped)

1/8 teaspoon turmeric powder

salt to taste

For tempering:

1 tablespoon sesame oil

1/2 teaspoon mustard seeds

4-5 green chillies (finely chopped) (adjust according to the heat of the chillies)

1 sprig curry leaves

For garnish: cilantro leaves/coriander leaves (finely chopped)

Method :

1. Heat a wide pan/kadai with oil and temper with ingredients given under 'for tempering'.

2. Add chopped onions, tomatoes, peas, capsicum , moringa leaves, turmeric powder and salt.

Chef tip: The bread already has salt so add only for the vegetables.

3. Mix well over low flame and let the tomatoes become mushy.

4. Now add the chopped bread pieces , mix well .

5. Partially cover the pan and allow it to cook over low flame , occasionally stirring the upma .

Chef tip: If you like your upma crunchy and more tasty, you can add a teaspoon of ghee/clarified butter on the sides of the pan and continue cooking.

6. The cooking time will depend upon the texture of the upma you like. It will take approximately 7-8 minutes for medium crunchy bread upma.

7. Switch off and garnish with cilantro leaves.

You can serve it as is or with tomato ketchup.

15

Oats Upma

Ingredients

1. Oats - 1/2 cup
2. Rava /sooji - 1/4 cup
3. Onion -1
4. Green chilli - 1 finely chopped
5. Ginger- 1 inch piece finely chopped
6. Mixed vegetables - 1 cup (little of carrot, beans, capsicum, peas)
7. Water- 3/4 cup
8. Salt as required

For the seasoning

1. Oil - 1 tbsp
2. Mustard seeds -1 tsp
3. Hing- a pinch
4. Urad dal- 1/2 tsp
5. Red chilli -1
6. Curry leaves-few

Preparation:

Dry roast oats for a few minutes, until it becomes slightly hot to touch. Dry roast rava also.

Heat oil in a pan, add mustard seeds, when it splutters, add the rest of the ingredients mentioned under seasoning.

Add finely chopped onions, chilli, ginger and saute till onions turn slightly brown

Add all the vegetables, saute for a few minutes, then add 3/4 cup of water and salt required.

When water comes to boil, simmer the flame, add rava stirring continuously and cook till it is half done.

Then add oats, cover and cook till done. (oats need less time and less water to get cooked, so you can add it, after rava is half cooked)

Eat it with any chutney, or simply curd.

16

Masala Poha

Preparation time : 5 minutes

Cooking time : 10 minutes

Serves : 4

1 cup = 250 ml

Ingredients :

3 cups poha/beaten rice/aval

1 onion (finely chopped)

2 tomatoes (finely chopped)

1/4 cup peas

1/4 green bell pepper (capsicum, optional)

100 gms paneer /cottage cheese (cubed)

1/4 teaspoon turmeric powder

1/4 teaspoon all spice powder or garam masala

salt to taste

For tempering :

1 tablespoon sesame oil

1/2 teaspoon mustard seeds

1/4 teaspoon urad dal/split and husked black gram

10-12 groundnuts

1/2 " ginger (grated)

4 green chillies (finely chopped, adjust according to heat of the chilli)

1 sprig curry leaves

For garnish :

cilantro leaves (finely chopped)

2 tablespoons fresh coconut (grated, optional)

2 teaspoons of Sev /mixture

Method :

1. Wash poha twice, drain and set it aside.

(If you are using the thicker variety of poha, then after washing, soak in water for 3-4 minutes , so that they are soft but not mushy.)

2. Heat a pan with oil and temper with ingredients given under ' for tempering'.

3. Once tempered add the onions, tomatoes, peas ,salt, turmeric powder and mix well .

4. Cook over low flame till the tomatoes breakdown and become mushy.

5. Now add the paneer, capsicum, garam masala and mix well.

6. Immediately add the soaked and drained poha and keep mixing over low to medium flame.

7. Cover and cook for 5 minutes.

8. Stir well and switch off.

9. Garnish with cilantro,coconut, sev.

17

Tomato Rice

Ingredients needed

1. Rice -1 cup
2. Ripe tomatoes -4
3. Onion -2 medium size
4. Green chillies -2
5. Ginger-Garlic paste -1 tsp
6. Chillie Powder -1 tsp
7. Turmeric Powder -1/4 tsp
8. Salt as required
9. Oil -2 tbsp

For the seasoning

Mustard - 1/4 tsp, Asafoetida - a pinch, Curry leaves - little

Method: Soak Rice for 20 minutes. Drain water and pressure cook rice adding 2 cups of boiling water. Take juice of 4 tomatoes in a blender and keep it aside.

Heat 2 tbsp of oil in a kadai and add the ingredients for seasoning. Add onions and saute till it turns translucent. Add green chillies and ginger-garlic paste. Saute for a few more minutes. Then add tomato juice, turmeric powder, chillie powder and salt. Cook till oil separates. Add the cooked rice to the tomato gravy and mix well.

Garnish with coriander leaves. Eat with papads, potato chips or raita

18

Lemon Rice

Ingredients needed

1. Rice -1 cup
2. Lemon -1 (juicy one)
3. Cashew nuts- 5 -6
4. Salt to taste
5. Oil - 3 tsp

For the seasoning

1. Mustard -1/2 tsp/ Urad dal -1 tsp/ Channa dal -1 tsp
2. Red Chillies -1/ Green chillies -2
3. Finely chopped ginger-1 tsp
4. Turmeric Powder -1/4 tsp
5. Asafoetida -A pinch
6. Curry leaves -little

Method: Cook rice. Spread it in a plate, mix a tsp of sesame seed oil to it, so that the grains will not stick together. Heat oil, add mustard seeds, when mustard splutters , add urad dal, channa dal, red chillies and asafoetida .When dal turns slightly brown ,add green chillies, ginger, turmeric powder and curry leaves.

Squeeze lemon juice in a cup, add salt to it. Mix and add to the rice. Add the seasoning to the rice and mix well. Add more lemon juice if required. Add roasted cashew nuts and eat with potatoes curry.

19

Corn Mushroom Fried Rice

Ingredients:

1. Boiled Ćorn kernels - 1 cup (200 ml)
2. Sliced Mushrooms - 1 cup
3. Green Chillies -4 to 5 (with just a slit)
4.Onion - 1 large - thinly sliced
5.Ginger garlic paste -2 tsp
6. Basmati rice -2 cups
7. Water - 2 cups

Flavouring:

1. Bay leaves -2
2.Star Anise -1
3. Badi Elaichi/ Black Cardamom -1
4. Green cardamom -1
5. Cinnamon - 2 cm stick
6.Chilli powder - 1 tsp (adjust)
7. Dhania powder / Coriander powder - 1 tsp
8. Salt to taste
9. Ghee/ Clarified Butter - 3 tbsp
10. Chopped Cilantro leaves for garnish (optional)

METHOD:

1. Wash and soak basmati rice in water with the flavouring spices (except salt,chilli and dhania powder) for 15 minutes and cook till just done. Do not over cook.

2. In a heavy bottom wide pan or a deep and wide wok, heat ghee.

3. Add the ginger garlic paste and mix with ghee for 30 seconds. Add the onions green chillies and cook till translucent. You can add salt so that they

do not burn.

4. Now add the mushroom and let it cook on medium flame for 5 to 7 minutes. Mushroom cooks fast.

5. Once mushrooms are done add boiled corn,chilli powder, dhania powder and mix well. Let it cook for another 2 minutes in low flame.

6. Switch off and add the cooked rice.

7. Mix well. Once you have mixed well, switch on the flame and fry the rice in high flame continously stirring it for 5 to 7 minutes.

8. Garnish and serve hot with Raita and pappadom.

20

Flattened Rice (Aval, Doha)

Ingredients needed

1. Aval - 1 cup
2. Onion - 1 finely chopped
3. Ginger - 1 inch piece finely chopped
4. Green chillies - 1 finely chopped
5. Potato -1 (cubed boiled potatoes)
6. Turmeric powder - a pinch
7. Salt to taste
8. Lemon juice -1 tbsp

For the seasoning

Mustard -1 tsp/ Curry leaves - little

Method: Wash aval under running water for 2-3 minutes and put it in a sieve to drain all the water. Keep it aside. Heat a tsp of oil in a pan, add mustard seeds,curry leaves and when mustard splutters, add onions and saute till it turns transparent. Then add ginger, green chillies, turmeric powder and saute for a few more seconds. Add cubed boiled potatoes. Add salt to taste.

Add the Aval, lemon juice and mix well. Garnish with coriander leaves

21

Rava Dosa

Rava dosa is quick and easy to prepare. It needs no grinding or fermenting. Here is the simple and tasty dosa recipe.

Ingredients needed

1. Rava – 1/2 cup
2. Rice flour – 1/2 cup
3. All purpose flour/maida –1/4 cup
4. Water - 3 - 3 1/2 cups
5. Green Chillies - 1 finely chopped
6. Ginger – 1 inch piece
7. Whole black pepper – 1 tsp/ Cumin seeds –1 tsp
8. Salt as required

For the seasoning

Mustard – 1/2 tsp/ Asafoetida – a generous pinch/ Curry leaves- a little

Method: Soak Rava in a little buttermilk for 1 hour. Then mix rice flour, maida and water with it. The batter should be thin and watery. Add finely chopped ginger, finely chopped chillies, cumin seeds, whole black pepper and salt.

Heat a tsp of oil, add the ingredients for seasoning and pour it over the batter.

Heat a non stick tawa, take a little batter in a ladle and start filling it from the outer corners of the tawa to the inside in a net like pattern. Pour a tsp of oil around the dosa. Cover it with a lid, when it becomes golden brown, flip it over to the other side and let it get cooked.

Eat hot with any chutney or sambar of your choice.

22

Bread Dosai

Makes : 10 dosas/ 1 cup = 250 ml cup

Ingredients :

4 bread slices

1/4 cup rice flour

1 tablespoon rava/semolina/cream of wheat

1 tablespoon curd

1/2 teaspoon peppercorns (coarsely crushed)

1/2 teaspoon cumin seeds /jeera (coarsely crushed)

1 green chilli (finely chopped)

2 teaspoons sesame oil (for drizzling)

1 and 1/2 cup water (adjust)

salt to taste

Method :

1. In a mixer /food processor , tear and add the bread slices, rice flour , curd and grind it to a fine batter adding water little at a time.

2. Transfer it to a vessel, add rava, green chilli, peppercorns , cumin seeds, salt and adjust the water quantity so that the batter is neither too thick or too thin.

3. Allow it to rest for 15 minutes.

4. Heat a tava and when it is screamed hot, pour the batter around the tava till all the gaps are filled.

5. Once the dosai starts to crisp, you can fold the dosai and serve .

Note : No need to flip and cook the dosai.

23

Kadalai Mavu Dosai

INGREDIENTS

Besan (Kadalai Mavu) flour – 1 cup
Red Chilli Powder – 1/2 teaspoon
Turmeric Power – 1/4 teaspoon
Asafoetida Powder – 1/4 teaspoon
Green Chilli (small size) – 1
Coriander Leaves – few
Onion – 1
Tomato – 1
Salt – 1/2 teaspoon or as per taste
Oil – 4 teaspoons

Method

Chop onion, tomato, green chilli and coriander leaves finely.

In a bowl put Besan, red chilli powder, turmeric, asafotida, salt and mix well. Add required water and make batter like dosa batter. Add chopped green chilli and coriander leaves to the batter and mix it well.

Heat a non-stick tawa and pour a big ladle of the batter starting from the corner to the middle of the tawa (like making rawa dosai). Lift the Tawa and tilt in a circular motion so that the batter spreads uniformly. Sprinkle chopped onion and tomato on the top. Pour little oil around the dosa and allow to cook for few minutes. Flip it over and cook other side also and remove.

Serve with any chutney.

24

Paneer Masala Dosai

1 cup = 250 ml cup

Ingredients : 4 cups Dosa batter

For the paneer masala:

1 onion (finely chopped)

1 tomato (finely Chopped)

1/4 cup fresh peas (shelled)

200 gm paneer/cottage cheese (grated)

1/4 teaspoon kashmiri chilli powder (for the vibrant colour)

salt to taste

To be ground (raw):

2 tomatoes

3 green chillies

1 garlic

1/2 " ginger

For tempering :

2 teaspoons oil

1/2 teaspoon mustard seeds

1 sprig curry leaves

For garnish : finely chopped cilantro or mint leaves

Method :

1. Heat a pan with oil and temper with ingredients given.
2. Add the ground paste.
3. Mix well, add salt and fresh peas.
4. Let the peas cook in the ground paste for 2-3 minutes.
5. Add kashmiri chilli powder and the finely chopped onion and tomatoes.

6. Let them cook for another 2-3 minutes.

Note: Keep stirring over low/medium flame.

7.Now add the grated paneer, mix well and cook for another 5 minutes and switch off.

8. Make dosa like the regular dosai.

9. Once the dosai is cooked, spread the paneer masala, fold and serve.

25

Egg Roll

INGREDIENTS

1. EGGS- 2
2. Finely chopped bell peppers
3. Finely chopped parsley or cilantro
4. Salt to taste
5. Black pepper/ chilli flakes(adjust to taste)
6. Oil for greasing

1. Beat the eggs well. Now sieve the eggs. This is the main difference...yes,it does make a difference. Add salt and pepper.

2. Cut the vegetables.

3. Heat the Greased pan.

4. Now pour one ladle of egg mixture and move the pan with your hand to spread the batter evenly, Sprinkle the veggies.

5. Cook only on one side.Transfer the egg crepe into a plate.

6.Roll the crepe tightly with the yellow side facing upwards. Using a pizza cutter cut then into 5 cm rolls.

7. Arrange them in a plate and serve hot with toast! It looked so gorgeous,delicate and soft!

26

Mint Pasta

Preparation time :10 minutes

Cooking time : 20 minutes

Serves :2

Measurement : 1 cup =250ml

Vessel required : Medium sized heavy bottom pan

Ingredients :

1. Pasta - 2 cups
2. Butter (unsalted) - 3 tablespoon
3. Mint leaves -a bunch (30 to 40 leaves approx.)
4. Garlic - 3 (large)
5. Ripe Tomatoes -4 large
6. Chilli Flakes - 1 teaspoon
7. Olive Oil - 1 teaspoon
8. Salt- to taste
9. Apple Cidar Vinegar - 1 tsp

METHOD :

1. Add the pasta to boiling water and cook for approximately 9 to 11 minutes. Add 1/4 tsp of salt to the water.

2. When the pasta is just cooked ' Al Dente ' drain the pasta in a colander and add the remaining olive oil and mix to coat the oil.

3. While boiling the pasta, you can also blanch the tomatoes ,remove seeds and chop them roughly.This saves you time.

4. Process the butter and garlic in a mixer or mortar and pestle to make a paste.

5. Chop the mint leaves.

6. Place a heavy bottom pan on the gas stove. And over medium flame, add the garlic butter mixture.

7. Cook for half a minute and add the chopped mint leaves and saute' for just a minute.

8. Add tomatoes and vinegar and cook for another minute stirring continously.

9. Add the Chilli flakes and salt to taste.

10. Add the cooked pasta, mix well and simmer in low flame for 5 minutes and switch off.

Garnish with fresh mint leaves and serve with toasted bread. Yum!

Tips :

1. You can use Olive Oil if you have diet restrictions.
2. Use ripe tomatoes and fresh mint leaves.
3. Serve pasta hot.
4. You can garnish with dry oregano and grated cheese .
5. Cook in medium flame.
6. Adding salt in Pasta helps prevent the pasta from overcooking and retain shape. So do not omit.
7. Tossing the Pasta in olive oil helps to add flavour, contrary to the regular belief.

27

Egg dosa

Egg dosa is a healthy, filling and protein-packed breakfast. Egg spread on the dosa and seasoned with salt and pepper.

Ingredients

1/2 cup Dosa Batter

1 no Egg

1/2tsp Salt

1/4 tsp Black pepper powder

1 tsp Oil

Method

Heat a wide skillet and pour a ladle full of batter on the center a skillet and spread into a thin circle.

Crack open the egg on the dosa and break the yolk with a fork or spoon and spread evenly on the dosa.

Season with salt and crushed black peppers. Drizzle oil on the sides of a dosa and cook on both the sides until the egg and bottom side of the dosa get cooked thoroughly.

28

Adai dosa

Ingredients

1/2 cup MOONG DAL RAW
1/4 cup CHANNA DAL RAW
1/2 cup TOOR DAL
1 tbsp URAD DAL
1/2 cup IDLI RICE
1/4 tsp HING OR ASAFOETIDA
5 no DRY RED CHILIES
1 cup ONION CHOPPED
1 no GREEN CHILIES
1/2 cup BASMATI RICE or Rawrice
1 inch GINGER

Method

Wash and soak the idli rice, basmati rice, toor dal, channa dal, moong dal and urad dal together for 5 hours.

After 5 hours grind rice, lentils, ginger and red chilies together until smooth. Add water little by little and grind it to a smooth batter. The batter should not be too thick or thin.

Chop the onion and green chilies finely. In a wide bowl combine rice and lentils batter, chopped onion, green chilies, salt, and asafoetida together. Mix well.

In a hot skillet pour a ladle full of batter and spread it in a circular motion. Drizzle oil on sides of the dosa and cook until the bottom side turns crispy.

Flip and cook on the other side until the brown spots appear. Adai dosa is ready to be served and be delicious with coconut chutney or avial.

29

Moong Dal Dosa

Making batter

1. Firstly, rinse ½ cup whole moong beans and 2 tablespoons rice a couple of times in water. Then soak the moong beans and rice for 4 to 6 hours or overnight in enough water. Drain all the water.

2. In a blender or mixer-grinder, add the moong beans and rice after draining all the water. You can even rinse the moong beans and rice before grinding.

Add 1 green chilli (chopped), 2 tablespoons chopped coriander leaves, 1 inch ginger (chopped), ½ teaspoon cumin seeds, 1 pinch asafoetida (optional), salt as per taste and ⅓ to ½ cup water. Skip asafoetida for a gluten-free moong dal dosa.

3. Grind or blend to a smooth batter. The batter consistency is similar to that of a regular Dosa Batter.

Tip 1: If the batter looks thick, then add 1 to 2 tablespoons more water.

Tip 2: If the batter looks thin, then add 1 to 2 tablespoons rice flour. You can even add gram flour (besan).

4. On a cast iron tawa or skillet , smear some oil or ghee with a paper towel or with half of an onion. Keep the heat to low or medium-low when spreading the pesarattu batter.

With a big spoon, pour the batter on the griddle and use the same spoon for spreading the batter into a round shape. For a non-stick tawa or pan, do not spread oil on it.

5. Sprinkle some finely chopped onions, chopped green chilies (optional) and coriander leaves (optional).

Press these with the spatula so that they get stuck to the batter which is getting cooked. Drizzle oil at the sides and in the center.

6. Flip and cook the second side for a half a minute or a minute. This will just lightly cook the onions.

7. Fold and serve moong dal dosa.

8. Make all dosas this way with the rest of the batter. Serve hot or warm with ginger chutney or coconut chutney.

Tips

Can rice flour be added instead of rice?

Yes absolutely. Add 2 to 3 tablespoons rice flour.

Can I use any other flour instead of rice flour?

Yes, you can use chickpea flour (besan) or any flour like ragi or jowar flour. But note that these flours will contribute their taste in the recipe.

Can I skip rice?

Rice gives a crispy texture to the dosa. But you can skip adding rice in the recipe.

I am not fond of raw onions, so how can I use them in the recipe?

You could skip them completely. Or sauté onions until softened or light golden, top them on dosa once it is cooked. In some hotels, they follow this method and even sauté the onions in ghee (clarified butter).

Can I use leftover cooked moong dal in the pesarattu recipe?

No, this recipe cannot be made with cooked moong dal.

What is the soaking time for whole green mung beans vs split yellow mung beans?

Soak the green moong beans for 4 to 6 hours or overnight. The split yellow moong lentils can be soaked for 1 hour to 3 hours. Less time taken for soaking results in a more crisp texture.

Can I use moong sprouts to make this recipe?

Yes, you can easily use moong sprouts to make this. Grind the mung sprouts to a fine batter with the other ingredients mentioned in the recipe.

Can I add cream of rice instead of rice flour?

Yes, you can add cream of rice (idli rava) instead of rice flour.

Can I refrigerate the moong dal dosa batter?

You can refrigerate the batter, but the texture and taste changes when you make dosa.

30

Ragi Dosa

Making batter

1. Take 1 cup ragi flour (finger millet flour) and ¼ cup besan (gram flour) in a mixing bowl or pan. You can even use rice flour or chickpea flour instead of besan.

2. Add the following ingredients:

⅓ to ½ cup finely chopped onions

½ teaspoon finely chopped ginger

8 to 10 curry leaves (chopped)

1 green chilli (chopped)

3 tablespoons chopped coriander leaves

1 pinch asafoetida (hing)

½ teaspoon cumin seeds

salt as per taste

3. Add ½ cup buttermilk and 1.5 cups water. To make the buttermilk, stir briskly ¼ cup curd (yogurt) with ¼ cup water.

TIP: You can also use the buttermilk obtained after churning butter.

4. Mix to a thin batter.

5. Add 3 tablespoons fresh grated coconut. (optional) Mix very well. Cover and let the batter rest for 15 to 20 minutes.

Making Ragi Dosa

6. Heat a cast-iron or non-stick tawa/skillet on medium heat. Spread some oil on the tawa.

7. Before pouring batter mix very well as the flours settle on the bottom of the pan. On the medium hot tawa or skillet pour the batter from outside to inside just like you do for Rava Dosa.

Then you can gently spread the batter with the ladle. If there are some empty spots, then pour a bit of the batter in the spots to cover it.

8. Let the base cook and become crisp. Sprinkle some oil on top and spread it with a spoon. Sprinkle a few drops of oil on the sides as well.

9. When the base is golden and crisp, turn over and cook the other side. Cook till both sides are crisp and cooked well. Make all ragi dosa this way.

10. Serve ragi dosa hot or warm.

Serving Suggestions

Serve ragi dosa with a potato masala (potato bhaji), any Indian veggie stir-fries, sambar or coconut chutney.

Tips

Sourness: If you do not like the sourness in dosa due to the buttermilk being added, then you can add a bit of milk in combination with the buttermilk. For more sourness you can use sour curd.

Replacing gram flour: You could even add rice flour instead of the besan (gram flour) in this ragi dosa recipe.

Spicing it up: I have added chopped onions, green chillies, ginger to the batter to make it more wholesome and spicier. You can easily skip the onions, herbs and spices and make dosa just with ragi, besan, buttermilk and salt.

Coconut: If you do not have fresh coconut, then you can add desiccated coconut or skip it completely.

Sprouted ragi flour can be used instead of ragi flour.

Fermented Ragi Dosa

Soaking rice and lentils

1. Take 1 cup idli rice or parboiled rice (ukda chawal, sela chawal) in a bowl.

2. Rinse the rice a couple of times. Add 1 to 1.5 cups water and keep the rice aside.

3. Rinse ¼ cup thick poha (flattened rice) once or twice and add to the rice bowl. Mix very well. Cover and keep aside to soak for 4 to 5 hours.

4. In another bowl take ½ cup urad dal and ¼ teaspoon fenugreek seeds (methi).

5. Rinse both for a couple of times. Then soak both the urad dal with the fenugreek seeds in 1 cup water for 4 to 5 hours.

Making Batter

6. After 4 to 5 hours, drain the urad dal and add in a mixer-grinder jar. Also add water in parts.

7. Grind the urad dal and methi seeds until you get a smooth and fluffy batter. While grinding, add water in parts. Once the batter is ground well, then pour the urad dal batter in a bowl or pan.

8. Next drain the rice, poha and add them to the same mixer-grinder jar. Depending on your jar capacity, you can grind the rice in two to three batches.

9. Grind the rice till smooth or a fine granular consistency in the batter is also fine. While grinding, if the mixer-grinder becomes hot, then stop. Once the grinder cools down, then continue to grind.

10. Pour the rice batter in the same bowl containing the urad dal batter.

11. Mix both the batters very well.

12. Now add 1 cup ragi flour (nachni or finger millet flour).

13. Then add ½ cup of water. You can adjust the water amount here depending on the consistency of the batter.

14. Mix very well with a wired whisk or spoon or with your hands. Break the lumps if any. Mix to a smooth batter.

A bit of handwork is required while mixing the ragi flour with the dosa batter.

Alternatively, you could mix the ragi flour in ½ cup water (preferably warm) in a separate bowl. Then add this ragi batter to dosa batter. There would be no lump formation this way and also less strain while mixing.

15. Cover the bowl or pan with a lid and let it ferment overnight or for 8 to 9 hours or more depending on the temperature conditions in your city. The batter will increase in volume and double up.

16. The ragi dosa batter after fermentation on the next day. if the batter does not increase in volume, then just add ¼ teaspoon baking soda in the batter. Mix very well and then proceed to make ragi dosa or idli.

17. Add salt and mix very well. I added salt the next day due to it being a cold season here. In a warmer climate, add salt before you keep the batter for fermentation.

Cooking Ragi Dosa

18. Heat an iron skillet or tawa or a non-stick pan. Dip half of an onion in oil and smear the oil on the iron tawa or griddle. If using non-stick pan, then don't smear oil.

19. Pour a ladle of the batter and quickly spread the dosa with the help of ladle in a circular motion.

20. Let the one side cook. Drizzle with ½ to 1 teaspoon oil on the top and sides.

21. Flip and cook the other side of nachni dosa till crisp and browned. instead of cooking the dosa on both sides, you can just cook one side.

22. When both the sides are cooked and crisp, remove the dosa.

23. Serve this healthy fermented ragi dosa hot or warm. Any leftover batter can be refrigerated for a couple of days or frozen for about a month.

Serving suggestions

Like regular dosa, these ragi dosa also go well with coconut chutney and sambar or even idli-dosa podi (dry chutney).

31

Coconut Chutney

Here is the recipe for Coconut chutney which goes well with Idly, Dosa, Pongal, etc.

Ingredients needed

1. Coconut - 3/4 cup (grated)
2. Green chillies - 3
3. Fried Gram -1 tbsp (pottukadalai)
4. Ginger - small piece
5. Salt to taste

For the seasoning

Mustard -1/4 tsp

Urad dal - 1/4 tsp

Curry leaves - a little

Method: Grind the above ingredients in the Mixie with enough water and salt. Heat a tsp of oil and add the ingredients for seasoning and season the chutney. For red coconut chutney, use red chillies instead of green chillies.

32

Tomato Chutney

Tomato chutney is a good combination for idly, dosa, chappati and also bread. Instead of butter or jam, you can use this chutney as a spread.

Ingredients needed

1. Ripe tomatoes - 4
2. Onion - 1 medium sized
3. Red chillies - 4 -5
4. Curry leaves - handful
5. Oil - 3 tbsp
6. Salt as required

Ingredients for seasoning

Mustard-1/2 tsp

Urad dal-1/2 tsp

Curry leaves -little

Method

Heat 3 tsp of oil and saute red chillies and curry leaves.

Then add chopped onions and saute for a few minutes.

Add chopped tomatoes. After it is half cooked, remove from flame.

Add salt needed. Cool it and grind it. Do not add water.

Heat 2 tbsp of oil in a kadai and add the ingredients for seasoning.

Add the grounded chutney to the kadai and cook again for 3-4 minutes till the oil separates.

33
EGG THOKKU

Egg thokku is an easy and quick side dish that serves with chapati and rice. It tastes spicy and flavorful with spices, tomatoes.

Ingredients:

1. Onion (big)-1
2. Tomatoes (big)- 3
3. Redchilli powder(or Sambar powder)- 2 tb spoon
4. Turmeric powder- 1/4 teaspoon
5. Salt for taste
6. Coriander leaves for garnishing
7. Eggs as per requirement.

Tempering:

1. Mustard seeds- 1 teaspoon
2. curry leaves 10

HOW TO MAKE PERFECT HARD BOILED EGGS?

Hard boiled eggs are a quick and cheapest source of protein. You can serve the boiled eggs for breakfast, snack or as a side with rice varieties like tomato rice and pulao. Hard boiled are simple to make in few minutes boil and stays good in the refrigerator for up to a week.

1. In a saucepan place eggs in a single layer, add water to cover the eggs, add a pinch of salt and bring to a vigorous boil. Turn off the heat and cover the pan with a lid.
2. Allow the eggs to sit in the hot water for 15 minutes. Drain the water from eggs completely, crack open the eggs and serve.

METHOD:

1. Heat the pan and add 3 table spoon cooking oil, and add mustard seeds, after spluttering add curry leaves and add finely chopped onion, saute well

with little salt on it.

2. Once the onion becomes glossy, add tomatoes and cook thoroughly until soft and mushy. If the tomatoes remain uncooked then the gravy will taste raw tomato flavor.

(The tomatoes can be finely chopped or made in to puree.)

3. After the tomatoes becomes mushy and oil splits out add turmeric and chilli powder and required salt and saute well, if required add 1/3 cup water, and bring to boil.

Don't add more water, the consistency should be thick gravy.

4. Now add the eggs (whole or Cut into pieces) and mix gently.

5. Finally add finely chopped coriander leaves and switch off the stove.

Goes well with sambar rice, Rasam rice, chapatti, dosa, etc.

34

Egg pepper fry

Ingredients

2 no EGG WHL RAW FRSH
1 cup ONIONS RAW
1/2 tsp CORIANDER POWDER
1 tsp GINGER GARLIC PASTE
1/4 tsp PEPPER BLACK
1/2 tsp SALT TABLE
3 tbsp OIL

Method

Place eggs in saucepan with cold water, enough to cover the eggs.

Bring the water to boil, remove from heat and cover the pan. Let eggs stand in hot water for 12 minutes.

Discard the water and crack open the eggs and slice it.

In a separate pan heat oil add fennel seeds, sliced onion, curry leaves and cook until onions become soft.

Add ginger garlic paste and cook until it loses its raw smell.

Add salt, coriander powder, pepper powder and mix well.

Add sliced eggs and mix gently and serve.

35

Pepper Chicken

This chicken recipe is a great soothing recipe for common cold and flu.

Ingredients

1.50 lb CHICKEN

1 tsp PEPPER BLACK

1/2cup OIL/ 10 no CURRY LEAVES

2 cup ONION CHOPPED

1/2 tbsp SALT TABLE

1/2 tbsp RED CHILI POWDER

1/2 tbsp CORIANDER POWDER

1.50 tbsp GARAM MASALA

1 tbsp GINGER GARLIC PASTE

1/4 tsp TURMERIC POWDER

1 tsp FENNEL SEED/1 tsp PEPPER BLACK

1/4 cup CILANTRO (CORIANDER)LEAVES RAW

4 no GREEN CHILIES

Method

Chop the chicken into small pieces and slice the onions thinly. In a pan heat oil, add in the fennel seeds, curry leaves, green chilies, sliced onion and cook until onion becomes soft.

Add the turmeric powder, ginger garlic paste, mix well and cook until the ginger garlic paste loses its raw smell.

Add the chopped chicken pieces, coriander powder, red chili powder, salt, garam masala and mix well. Cover and cook, until chicken, get cooked thoroughly over a medium heat. Make sure to stir in between to avoid burning the onions and spices.

Take off the lid and mix in the crushed whole black pepper and stir fry for 5 min. Garnish it with chopped coriander leaves.

36

Cabbage with moong dal

Ingredients

4 cup CABBAGE RAW CHOPPED
1 cup ONION CHOPPED
2 no GREEN CHILIES/3 tbsp OIL
1/4 cup COCONUT GRATED
1/2 tsp MUSTARD SEEDS
1/2 tsp URAD DAL/10 no CURRY LEAVES
1/4 tsp TURMERIC GROUND
4 tbsp MOONG DAL RAW
1 tsp SALT TABLE/1/4 cup WATER

Method

Soak moong dal in hot water for 10 minutes (use little amount of hot water to soak the moong dal, drain the dal from hot water and reserve 1/4 cup of water from it, so that you can use it for cooking the cabbage and you don't want to miss the nutrition from the dal by discarding the water).

Chop the cabbage, onion and green chilies finely.

In a pan heat oil add mustard seeds and allow it to splutter. Add urad dal, curry leaves, onion, green chilies and cook until onion becomes soft., Add turmeric powder and mix well. Cook until the turmeric powder loses its raw smell.

Add chopped cabbage, soaked moong dal, salt, water and mix well. Cover and cook until cabbage become soft (keep stirring in between to avoid burning the cabbage).

Add shredded coconut and mix well. Turn off from the heat and transfer it to a serving bowl.

37

POTATO FRY

Ingredients

2 no POTATOES
4 tbsp OIL
1 tsp RED CHILI POWDER
2 tsp CORIANDER POWDER
3/4 tsp SALT TABLE
1/2 tsp MUSTARD SEEDS
1 tsp URAD DAL
1/4 tsp HING OR ASAFOETIDA
10 no CURRY LEAVES
1/2 tsp BLACK PEPPER POWDER

Method

Chop the potatoes into small pieces. In a pan heat oil add mustard seeds and allow it to splutter.

Add urad dal and cook until the colour changes into golden brown. Add asafoetida and mix well in the oil. Add curry leaves, chopped potatoes and mix well

Cover and cook until potatoes become soft, but not mushy.

Add red chili powder, salt, turmeric powder, coriander powder and mix well

Cook uncovered until the potatoes turn crispy. Keep stirring in between to avoid potatoes get burned.

Add pepper powder, mix well and serve.

38
EGGPLANT CURRY

Ingredients

5 no EGGPLANT
4 no ROMA TOMATO/1 no ONIONS CHOPPED
1 tbsp GARLIC RAW/5 tbsp OIL
1/2 tsp FENUGREEK SEED
1/2 tsp MUSTARD SEEDS
1 tsp URAD DAL/10 no CURRY LEAVES
40 gms TAMARIND
1 tbsp CORIANDER POWDER
1 tsp PEPPER RED OR CAYENNE
1/4 cup COCONUT MEAT RAW
1/2 tsp CUMIN SEED

Method

Slice the eggplants (brinjal) and chop the onion, garlic, and tomatoes finely. Soak tamarind in warm water for 10 minutes and extract the tamarind juice. Keep aside.

In a pan heat oil add mustard seeds and wait until it gets splutter. Add fenugreek seeds, urad dal, asafoetida, curry leaves, chopped garlic, onion and cook until onion becomes soft.

Add sliced eggplant and cook until it gets cooked completely. Add chopped tomatoes and cook until it becomes soft.

Add coriander powder, salt, turmeric powder, red chili powder and mix well. Cook until the spices lose its raw smell.

Add the tamarind extract and allow it to boil for 5 - 7 minutes. Grind shredded coconut and cumin seeds together to a smooth paste and add it to the curry. Mix well and garnish it with chopped coriander leaves.

39

Avial

Avial is a popular dish in Kerala made with mixed vegetables, coconut, and yogurt. It is an easy and simple side dish to make in 30 minutes.

Ingredients

100 gms GREEN BEANS

100 gms CARROTS RAW

75 gms POTATO

1/4 cup SHREDDED COCONUT

2 tbsp PLAIN YOGURT

1 no GREEN CHILIES

1/2 tsp CUMIN SEED

1 tsp SALT TABLE

1/4 tsp TURMERIC POWDER

1/2 cup WATER

1 tsp COCONUT OIL/5 no CURRY LEAVES

Method

Peel and chop the potato, carrot and green beans into small pieces.

In a blender or mixer grind the shredded coconut, cumin seeds, and green chilies together until smooth and keep it aside until needed.

In a pan add chopped potato, green beans, carrot, salt, water and turmeric powder. Cover and cook until the vegetables get 3/4 done.

Uncover the lid and add the grounded coconut mixture. Cover and cook until the vegetables become soft (but not mushy). (You should taste each and every piece of the vegetable in avial).

Add yogurt and mix well. Check for the salt and remove from a heat immediately.

In a small skillet heat coconut oil, add curry leaves and add it to the avial.

40

Onion Pakoda

INGREDIENTS

Instant Bajji/Bonda Mix – 100 gram
Onion – 2
Fresh ginger – a small piece
Garlic flakes – 2
Aniseeds/fennel – 1/2 teaspoon
Curry leaves – few
Oil – for deep frying

Method

Chop onion into lengthwise thin slices. Chop ginger and curry leaves finely. Crush garlic flakes.

In a broad vessel put the Instant Bajji/Bonda Mix. Add the chopped onion, ginger, curry leaves and crushed garlic flakes. Add aniseeds, pinch of salt and mix well. Sprinkle little water and knead it to hard dough.

Heat oil in a Kadai. Take the dough and pinch it into small pieces and put it in the hot oil. Fry till it become golden brown.

Goes well with Sambar Rice / plain pulao or serve it as evening snack with tea.

41

Green Peas Masala

INGREDIENTS

Green Peas – 1 cup

Cashew Nuts – 5

Curd – 2 tablespoons

Red Chilli Powder – 1/2 teaspoon

Turmeric Powder – 1/4 teaspoon

Garam Masala Powder – 2 pinches

Salt – 1/2 teaspoon or as per taste

To fry and grind:

Big Onion – 1

Tomato – 1

Fresh Ginger – a small piece

Garlic Cloves (Small size) – 2

For Seasoning:

Oil – 2 tablespoons

Cumin Seeds – 1/2 teaspoon

Chopped onion – 2 tablespoons

Coriander Leaves chopped – 1 tablespoon

Method

Cook the green peas till soft.

Soak cashew nuts in warm water for about 10 to 15 minutes.

Chop onion, tomato, ginger and garlic roughly.

In a kadai put two teaspoons of oil. When it is hot add chopped onion and fry till it slightly changes its colour. Add ginger and garlic and fry for a while. Then add tomato and fry till it mashes well. Remove from stove and cool it.

Put the fried items, soaked cashew nuts and curd in a mixie jar. Grind it to a fine paste.

Put 1 tablespoon oil in a kadai and when it is hot add cumin.

Add chopped onion and fry for few seconds.

Add ground masala paste along with red chilli powder, turmeric powder, garam masala powder and salt. Mix well.

Add cooked peas and little water and make it semi liquid. Allow to boil.

Remove and garnish with coriander leaves and tomato slices.

Goes well with Chapati/plain pulao.

42

Kara Boondhi Kurma

INGREDIENTS

Kara Boondhi – 1 cup
Potato – 2 Nos
Big onion (medium size) – 1 No
Tomato – 1
Red Chilly Powder – 1/2 teaspoon
Coriander Powder – 1/2 teaspoon
Turmeric powder – ¼ teaspoon
Salt – 1 teaspoon or as per taste
To Grind
Coconut gratings – 2 tablespoon
Cashew nuts – 4 to 5 Nos
Puffed gram dhal (Pottu kadalai) – 1 teaspoon
Garlic cloves – 2 Nos
Fresh ginger – 1 " piece
Green Chillies – 1 to 2 Nos

For seasoning

Oil – 2 tablespoons
Fennel seeds – 1 teaspoon
Cinnamon stick – 1 small piece
Cardamom – 1
Cloves – 2

Method

Cook potato till soft and remove the skin. Cut it into medium size pieces. Chop onion and tomato finely.

Grind Coconut gratings, Cashew nuts, puffed gram dhal, Garlic cloves, Fresh ginger, Green Chillies, together to a fine paste.

In a kadai put the oil and when it is hot add cinnamon stick, cardamom, cloves and fennel seeds. When it is slightly fried, add chopped onion and fry till it turns transparent. Add tomato pieces along with salt, turmeric powder, red chilli powder, coriander powder and stir it. Fry till tomato mashed well. Now add potato pieces and mix well. Add the ground paste. Mix once again everything well and add enough water to cover the potato. Close with a lid and cook till it starts boiling. Allow to boil for few more seconds. Remove from stove, add kara boondhi and stir well.

Can be served with any mild pulao / Indian bread.

43

Rajma Curry

Ingredients:

1. 150 gms Kidney Beans (Rajma)
2. 2 medium sized Onion
3. 1 large Tomato
4. 2 Green chilli
5. 1 tblsp Ginger-garlic paste
6. 1/2 tspn Garam masala powder
7. 1 tsp Coriander (Dhania) powder
8. 3/4 tsp Salt

Preparation:

Soak the rajma overnight.

Boil in a pressure cooker till tender.

Heat oil in a pan and add the chopped onions and ginger garlic paste.

Cook till brown.

Add the tomatoes, green chillies and cook till pulpy.

Add coriander powder, salt and 2 cups water and boil well.

Add the rajma and cook on a low flame for about 10 minutes.

Add the garam masala powder and cook further for another 15 minutes or till the gravy thickens.

Garnish with coriander leaves.

Goes well with steamed rice or chapathi/ roti.

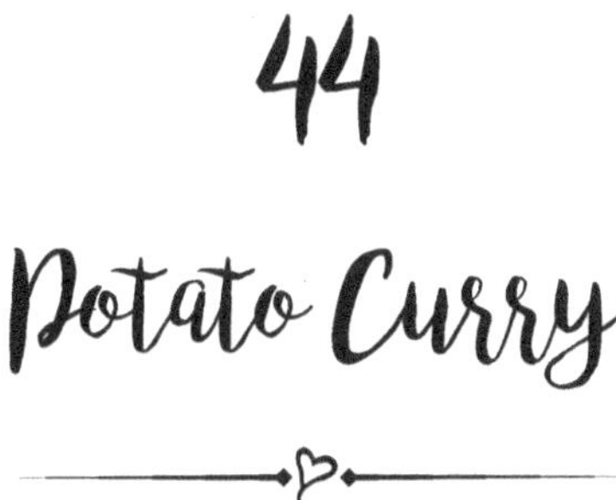

Ingredients needed

1. Potatoes -250 grams
2. Onion -1 big finely chopped
3. Ginger - 1 tbsp (finely chopped)
4. Green Chillie - 1 finely chopped
5. Turmeric powder - a pinch
6. Garam Masala powder -1 tbsp (you can also use plain chillie powder)
7. Salt as required
8. Oil -2 tbsp

For the seasoning

Mustard - 1/2 tsp/ Urad dal - 1/2 tsp/ Curry leaves - little

Method: Pressure cook potatoes. Peel the skin and cut it into big pieces.

Heat oil in a pan, add the ingredients for seasoning .When mustard splutters, add onion and saute well till it becomes transparent. Then add ginger, green chillies and saute for a few more minutes. Add the potatoes, turmeric powder, salt and Garam masala/ Chillie powder. Cook covered on low fire stirring from time to time to prevent the potatoes from getting burnt.

Note - Be a little generous in adding oil for the curry for a yummy taste.

45

Moong (Green Gram) Gravy

INGREDIENTS

Moong (Green Gram) – 1 cup

Big Onion – 1/Tomato – 1

Red Chilli Powder – 1/2 teaspoon

Turmeric Powder – 2 pinches

Vaangi Bath Powder or Pav Baji Masala Powder – 2 teaspoons

Oil – 1 tablespoon

Jeeragam (Cumin) – 1 teaspoon

Asafoetida powder – a pinch

Coriander leaves – few/Salt – 1 teaspoon or as per taste

Method

Soak Moong (Green Gram) in water for 6 to 8 hours.

Pressure cook for 2 to 3 whistles or till soft.

Chop onion and tomato finely.

In a kadai put the oil and when it is hot add jeeragam (cumin) and asafoetida powder. Add chopped onion and fry for few minutes. Add chopped tomato and fry till it mashes well. Add red chilli powder, turmeric powder and Vaangi Bath Powder (Or Pav Baji Masala Powder) and salt. Stir well for few seconds. Add cooked Moong (Green Gram) along with the water in which it is cooked. Allow to cook till it is thick and blends well with the masala.

Remove from stove and garnish with cut onion, Green chilli, tomato and coriander leaves.

This gravy goes well with Chapati or any Indian Bread. Can also be served with hot steamed rice/mild pulao.

46

Tomato Sweet Pachadi

INGREDIENTS

Tomato (medium size) – 3
Sugar – 3 tablespoons
Ghee – 1 teaspoon
Cashewnuts – few
Raisins – few
Cardamom Powder – a pinch

Method

In a vessel boil four to five cups of water. When it starts boiling, add the tomatoes and close with lid. Cook for three minutes. Switch off the oven. Gently take out the tomatoes from the water and allow to cool. Once it has cooled down, peel the skin and put it in a mixie and make a fine puree.

Put the puree in a vessel and add sugar. Stir continuously and bring to boil. When it starts boiling and become little thick, fry cashew nuts and raisins in a teaspoon of ghee and add it to the pachadi along with cardamom powder. Mix it and remove.

Goes well with chappati and bread toast.

47

Mixed Vegetable Curd Pachadi

INGREDIENTS

Cucumber – 1
Big Onion – 1
Tomato – 1
Carrot – 1
Coriander leaves – few
Green Chillies – 2 (Medium size)
Salt – 1/2 teaspoon or as per taste
Curd – one big bowl

Method

Remove the skin and seeds from cucumber and and cut it into tiny pieces. Remove skin from carrot and cut it also to the same size of cucumber pieces. Cut tomato and remove the seeds and inner portion. Cut it into small pieces. Slit the green clillies and remove the seeds and chop finely. Chop Coriander leaves and onion finely.

Beat the curd and add salt and put it in a bowl. Add all the cut vegetables in the curd and mix well.

Goes well with all types of biriyani, pulao and variety rice.

48

Carrot Kosumalli

INGREDIENTS

Carrot (Medium size) – 2
Green Gram Dhal – 1/2 small cup
Green Raw Mango gratings- 1 tablespoon
Green chillies – 2
Coriander leaves – few
Coconut gratings – 2 tablespoon
Lemon juice – 1 teaspoon
Oil – 1/2 teaspoon
Mustard – 1/2 teaspoon
Asafotida – a pinch
Curry leaves – few
Salt – 1/2 teaspoon or as per taste

"Kosumalli", also called as "Kosumbari" is prepared with mixing raw vegetables like carrot, cucumber, plantain stem pieces and soaked green gram dhal. It is prepared with single vegetable or with combination of two or three vegetables. Normally carrot kosumalli is served in almost all the South Indian Weddings.

Method

Soak green gram dhal in water for about one hour.

Wash and remove the skin from carrot. Grate it.

Chop coriander leaves.

Slit the green chillies lengthwise and remove the seeds. (This will reduce the hotness of the chillies and you can eat the chillies also).

Put carrot gratings, green chillies, chopped coriander leaves and mango gratings in a bowl. Add salt and mix well.

In a small kadai, put the oil and when it is hot add mustard. When it pops up add asafotida powder and currey leaves. Put this seasoning on the carrot mixture.

Drain the water from dhal and add the soaked dhal to the carrot mixture.

Add lemon juice, coconut gratings and mix everything gently.

Tips: Instead of grating the carrot, you can also cut it into thin strips. This way the carrot will be more crisp when you eat.

49

Green Chili Pachadi

This pachadi pairs well with Dhal Rice and curd rice.

INGREDIENTS

Green Chillies – 6 to 8
Tamarind – a small lemon size
Turmeric Powder – 1/4 teaspoon
Jaggery powdered – 1 tablespoon
Salt – 1 teaspoon or as per taste
To fry and grind:
Thuvar dhal – 1 teaspoon
Coriander seeds – 2 teaspoons
Rice – 1 teaspoon
Asafotida – small piece

For seasoning:

Oil – 1 tablespoon
Mustard – 1/2 teaspoon
Fenugreek – 1/2 teaspoon

Method

In a dry kadai put thuvar dhal, coriander seeds, rice and asafoetida one by one and fry till it turns light brown. Remove, cool it and grind it to a coarse powder.

Soak tamarind in water and squeeze out the juice and make it to two cups by adding required water.

Slit the green chillies lengthwise, keeping the top portion in tact.

In the kadai put two teaspoons of oil and add the green chillies. Fry on medium flame till its green colour disappear and turn pale. Remove and keep aside.

Same kadai put a teaspoon of oil and when it is hot add mustard. When it pops up add fenugreek and fry just for a second (ensure not to burn it). Then add tamarind water along with turmeric powder and salt. Bring to boil. When it starts boiling, add jaggery and the dhal powder. Stir it well. Allow to boil for few more seconds. Finally add the fried chillies and mix it well. Let it boil for few seconds. Then remove it.

50 Popcorn

This is one of my favourite and quick recipe to have on hand while watching TV or when friends surprise at home.

A pressure cooker will do to make this quick snack.

Ingredients:

1 cup dried corn (easily available in any store)
refined oil (as required)
salt (as required. lesser the better)

Preparation:

In a cup, mix dry corn, oil and salt. Make sure that whole corn is soaked in enough oil. Heat the pressure pan and add this mixture. Place a lid on top, upside down and shake it slightly to make sure that corn does not get burned. Once you hear the popping sound, hold it for few more seconds and remove from the fire. Your hot popcorn is ready.

You can add masala and or butter on top to add to the taste.

www.ingramcontent.com/pod-product-compliance
Lightning Source LLC
LaVergne TN
LVHW041233150826
845673LV00008B/2372

* 9 7 9 8 8 8 9 0 9 4 1 0 4 *